LOVE & LOVING

MATTERS OF FACT

LOVE &
LOVING

IRENA CHALMERS

AN IRENA CHALMERS BOOK

Longmeadow Press

**PREPARED FOR LONGMEADOW PRESS BY
IRENA CHALMERS BOOKS, INC.**

MANAGING EDITOR: **Carlotta Kerwin**
ASSISTANT TO THE EDITOR: **David Chestnut**
COPY EDITOR: **Linda Stern**
PICTURE EDITOR: **Lisa Sorensen**

——————

COVER DESIGN: **Karen Skelton**
ART DIRECTION AND DESIGN: **Helene Berinsky**

TYPESETTING: **Pica Graphics, Monsey, New York**

——————

LOVE & LOVING

Published by Longmeadow Press, 201 High Ridge Road, Stamford, Connecticut 06904. No part of this book may be reproduced or used in any form or by any means, electronic or mechanical, including photocopying, recording, or by an information storage and retrieval system, without permission in writing from the publisher.

ISBN 0-681-40697-6

Printed in the United States of America

0 9 8 7 6 5 4 3 2 1

MATTERS OF FACT

CONTENTS

PICTURE CREDITS

p. 8, 11, 19, 20, 26, 53, 57, 60 The New York Public Library Picture Collection 9, 29, 32, 36, 37, 41, 42 Culver Pictures, Inc. 13, 22, 40, 50 Cartoons by Mort Gerberg 39 Courtesy Martin Moskof & Associates, Inc.

PICTURE CONSULTANT: ILENE CHERNA BELLOVIN

CHAPTER 1

WHAT IS LOVE?

It is not possible to define love—but this has not stopped philosophers, poets, and just plain folks from trying to express what love means to *them*. The range of interpretation is as varied as the emotion itself.

A ROSE IS A ROSE

The word "love" is from the Old English *lufu*, connected with both the Sanskrit *lubh*—"to desire"—and the Latin *lubet*, "it pleases."

Love is an irresistible desire to be irresistibly desired.

ROBERT FROST

LEAVING NOTHING TO CHANCE

It could be said that Adam and Eve are the only couple who were truly made for each other.

First love is a kind of vaccination which saves a man from catching the complaint a second time.

HONORÉ DE BALZAC

UNTIL DEATH DO US PART

We once thought, rather romantically as it turns out, that when we fell in love, we were likely to remain in that charmed state, provided we treated each other well.

New research seems to show, on the contrary, that passionate love is a transient, primitive emotion that is kept alive largely by anxiety and fear, and that both passionate and companionate love diminish with time. Fortunately, for many couples there is usually enough companionate love to begin with to last until advanced old age. Even passionate love may make a fleeting comeback during times of stress or when a relationship is in danger.

Love is the triumph of the imagination over intelligence.

H.L. MENCKEN

PLAIN SPEAKING

When *People* magazine interviewed the writer Dave Barry, he volunteered this interesting information: "Men and women aren't called opposite sexes for nothing. In my book I reveal that women want to be loved, listened to, respected, needed, trusted, and held. Men want tickets to the World Series."

TURNAROUND

In the 17th century, the phrase "There's no love lost between them" meant that two people loved each other so much that they could not look at anyone else; it has since come to be used for people who can not stand each other.

WHERE THE RAINBOW BEGINS

TRUE BLUE

Blue has been the color of the true lover and the faithful servant since medieval times. It has been found to have a psychological calming effect and is associated with harmony and sincerity.

BLOOD RED

Red, of course, expresses energy, aggression, happiness, and sexual desire. Primitive peoples and children are especially attracted to red; so are *femmes fatales*. Crimson reds are passionate colors, and the darker, the more purple the passion.

PRETTY PINK

A deep rose pink signifies romantic love, both sexual and emotional, but the paler the pink, the less sensual, because white is the traditional color of purity and innocence.

NATURAL COLORS

Green, the color of vegetation, has powerful connections with fertility and magic—and hence with love. Yellow, the color of sunshine, signifies youth and hope.

There isn't any formula or method. You learn to love by loving.

ALDOUS HUXLEY

PROTECTIVE COLORING

The Puritans, who believed that bright colors incited lust, wore only black, gray, and white.

FAITHFUL FIDO

The phrase "cupboard love" comes from the fickle affection bestowed on the owner by a dog hoping to be fed. (The food, as the pooch well knows, is stored in the cupboard.) By extension, this term has come to imply that love has an ulterior motive.

However, the phrase has nothing to do with the declaration, "Love me, love my dog." It was St. Bernard who uttered those words, though he said them in canonical language. *Qui me amat, amat et canem meam*, quoth he. His dog, however, was a giver of brandy, not a beggar for biscuits.

Love, friendship, and religion are the source of the most violent passions in life.

DENIS DIDEROT

LEARNING LOVING

We mostly tend to love and marry people like ourselves or people who are like the parents we grew up with. As humans, we have a period of childhood dependence on our parents that is abnormally long for the animal world. During that time, we learn how to develop profound and lasting attachments. These attachments can help us form lasting relationships as adults, too, but some people become obsessed with one parent and seek out a love partner who is just like—or is totally unlike—Daddy (or Mommy), depending on their experiences.

AS NATURE MADE HER

Mrs. Hilton-Wilding-Todd-Fisher-Burton-Burton-Warner may have been married so many times partly because so many men fell in love with her beauty. The men, however, may not have known precisely why they were so smitten. Neurologically speaking, Elizabeth Taylor has the most symmetrical face ever known in art and in history. No matter which way the quadrants are drawn, her features are perfectly aligned.

IT'S ALL MICKEY MOUSE TO US

Why do we speak of puppy love and calf love, but not of kitten love or foal love? A lover may make sheep's eyes at his loved one, but once married, he is likely to be henpecked.

"It's not that I *enjoy* screaming and beating on my chest . . . I just *do* it. It's my genetic programming.

LOVE MAPS

According to Dr. John Money, director of the Psycho-hormonal Research Unit at Johns Hopkins, we all fall in love with a fantasy superimposed or projected onto a partner. Somewhere between five and eight years of age, each of us is imprinted with a pattern in the brain that determines whom we will find attractive and what kind of relationship we will consider ideal. This love map is partly genetic and partly based on our early experiences, rather like the imprinting that goes on in newborn animals.

Love is like the measles; we all have to go through it.

JEROME K. JEROME

WOMANLY DEFINITIONS OF LOVE

Love is a force. It is not a result; it is a cause. It is not a product; it produces. It is a power, like money, or steam, or electricity. It is valueless unless you can give something else by means of it.

ANNE MORROW LINDBERGH

Love is an expression and assertion of self-esteem, a response to one's own values in the person of another.

AYN RAND

A woman cannot love a man she feels to be her inferior; love without veneration and enthusiasm is only friendship.

GEORGE SAND

What is important is that one is capable of love. It is perhaps the only glimpse we are permitted of eternity.

HELEN HAYES

In love as in war, a fortress that parleys is half taken.

MARGUERITE DE VALOIS

MANLY DEFINITIONS OF LOVE

*Man's love is of man's life a thing apart,
'Tis woman's whole existence.*

BYRON

*I profess not to know how women's hearts
are wooed and won. To me they have always
been matters of riddle and admiration.*

WASHINGTON IRVING

*Of all the paths leading to a woman's love,
pity is the straightest.*

FRANCIS BEAUMONT

*Love is like the moon; when it does not
increase, it decreases.*

ALEXANDRE DE SÉGUR

*It is possible that a man can be so changed
by love as hardly to be recognized as the
same person.*

TERENCE

*I have enjoyed the happiness of the world; I
have lived and loved.*

SCHILLER

WORDS OF CAUTION

"When poverty comes in at the door, love flies out at the window." This saying, or words to the same dismal effect, is universal in many languages.

Love hides in the deep recesses of the brain itself—the only place on earth where we haven't yet established our control. The brain is a master everywhere but in its own house. That's what makes love so special and so elusive. That's why when you love someone, you never feel really in control. It's the brain's greatest challenge and greatest exhilaration. It's a merging of two minds—and the bodies they command—on a level of consciousness we don't begin to understand. Of all the many mysteries of the universe, love is probably the only one we'll never solve.

PHIL DONAHUE
The Human Animal

The man who loves only himself cannot, it is true, be accused of promiscuity in his affections, but he is bound in the end to suffer intolerable boredom from the inevitable sameness of the object of his devotion.

BERTRAND RUSSELL

Love does not consist in gazing at each other but in looking outward together in the same direction.

ANTOINE DE SAINT-EXUPÉRY

ON CHOOSING BETWEEN A FACIAL AND A NAUTILUS MACHINE

Exercise may be great for sculpting a beautiful body and attracting a mate but Barbara Cartland's advice to a fiftyish woman who asked whether she should concentrate on her face or her figure was, "Have a lovely face and sit down."

When the tennis ball soared high above,
Nellie rose to receive it like a dove,
But the strain of her reach
Caused her panties to breach
And her partner to cry out, "That's love!"

ANONYMOUS

CHAPTER 2

SHOWING YOU CARE

"How do I love thee? Let me count the ways," wrote Elizabeth Barrett to Robert Browning. Some of the ways we express our feelings are charming, quaint, touching, and even funny. Often, it is the simplest things that have special meaning, known only to those who give and those who receive.

GIFTS OF LOVE, MODERN STYLE

Overhead on a singles computer network: "If you really want to touch someone's heart, then buy a rose. After you get the rose, buy a nice cuddly teddy bear. Then put the rose in the arm of the teddy bear and give it to her (or him) as a gift.

"With this, who needs to say anything?"

A ROSE RESCUES A PRICKLY SITUATION

The Greek god Cupid, son of Venus, gave a rose to Harpocrates, the god of silence, begging him not to reveal her many love affairs. Gradually, the rose became the symbol of discreet silence. And it became the practice to hang a rose over a secret meeting. Eventually, roses were painted or sculpted on the ceilings of banquet rooms to remind guests that what was said while the wine was flowing must remain confidential. The Latin phrase *sub rosa* ("under the rose") has come to mean "in strict confidence." Remember that when you send a dozen roses to your one true love.

In life, actions speak louder than words, but in love, the eyes do.

SUSAN B. ANTHONY

LOVE TOKENS, OLD STYLE

In olden days, knights would joust with their ladies'
favors pinned to their helmets. Suitable items were
flowers, gloves, kerchiefs, veils, and even sleeves
(which in the Middle Ages were frequently detach-
able). Presumably, a lady planned her outfit in advance to have a token ready to bestow when the
knight rode up. But nobody tells which of them
brought along the pins.

SAY IT WITH FLOWERS

In Victorian times, it was customary to send to one's
true love a nosegay instead of a letter, because
flowers could speak freely when a lover could not.
Today, we send a card with a printed message
inside. We ask others to express our thoughts with
words we cannot find for ourselves.

PLOTTING WITH PANSIES

The flower to beware of is the pansy, which is the
blossom that Oberon persuaded Puck to use to
bewitch Titania and the lovers in *A Midsummer
Night's Dream*.

SOME FLOWER MEANINGS

The bouquet you send can have a hidden message:

AMARYLLIS—pride
ANEMONE—forsaken
ASTER—talisman of love
BEGONIA—dark thoughts, beware!
CHRYSANTHEMUM—cheerfulness and hope
CROCUS—youth and joy, inspiration of love
DAFFODIL—regard
DAHLIA—instability
DAISY—innocence
DAY LILY—coquetry
FERN—fascination
FORGET-ME-NOT—true love
FOXGLOVE—insincerity
FUCHSIA—good taste
GLADIOLUS—you pierce my heart
HYACINTH—sport and play
IRIS—faith
LILY—orange: hatred; white: sincerity
LILY OF THE VALLEY—purity
MARIGOLD—pain and grief
NARCISSUS—egotism and deceit
PEONY—healing
PETUNIA—anger and resentment
PHLOX—a proposal or a wish for sweet dreams
SNAPDRAGON—presumption
SNOWDROP—hope and consolation
SWEET PEA—goodbye
TULIP—the perfect lover
VERBENA—may you get your wish
VIOLET—modesty
ZINNIA—thoughts of absent friends

THE IMPERSONAL KISS

If you want to give a kiss without committing yourself, there is an alternative. You can send a bunch of long-stemmed roses—made entirely of chocolate!

OF LOVE AND XXXX

From where did the custom of putting crosses for kisses in a letter come? Possibly, from the old Catholic custom of marking a cross at the beginning of a blessing.

A TOKEN OF HIS ESTEEM

"My beloved one gave me such a lovely unexpected present," Queen Victoria wrote on February 10, 1846, the sixth anniversary of her wedding to Prince Albert, "a wreath, going right round the head. . . . It is entirely his own design. The leaves are of frosted gold, the orange blossoms of white porcelain and [there are] four little enamel oranges meant to represent our four children."

"It must be love. Last night he gave me a tip on some little money market fund at 18%."

STRINGS OF PEARLS

Pearls are almost as popular a love gift as diamonds. In the early 1900s, an amorous banker exchanged a mansion on New York's Fifth Avenue for a double-stranded pearl necklace to give to his lady love.

The fashion designer Calvin Klein had much the same idea. He recently purchased a secondhand pearl necklace for $1.1 million for his wife, Kelly. The previous owner was the late Duchess of Windsor.

Why is it no one ever sent me yet
One perfect limousine, do you suppose?
Ah no, it's always just my luck to get
One perfect rose.

DOROTHY PARKER

DIAMONDS ARE FOREVER

The diamond is *the* jewel that symbolizes love. The hardest substance known, it is made of pure carbon, and the best specimens are completely colorless. The name is derived from the Greek *adamas*, meaning "invincible." Diamonds are also said to guarantee married happiness, to prevent fear of darkness, and to "make one merry." You bet.

The significance of the diamond engagement ring is twofold. First, since it is the most indestructible of minerals, the diamond signifies that nothing will cause the union to break. Second, the custom of giving a ring to the betrothed was once a tangible demonstration to the father of the bride that more riches were to come.

NEVER LOOK BACK

One of the most poignant love stories from mythology is that of Orpheus, who sang so sweetly he held the woodland animals spellbound and could make even the heart of stone dance. Orpheus' beloved wife, Eurydice, was bitten by a snake and died. Determined to get her back, Orpheus descended into the underworld and charmed its ruler, Pluto, with his music. Pluto released Eurydice on the condition that Orpheus not look back at her until they reached earth once more. But Orpheus could not resist stealing just one glance to be sure she was behind him. Alas, her spirit vanished instantly—and forever.

A CASTING OF PEARLS

Jenny Dolly, a vaudeville star, was much loved by Gordon Selfridge, the London department-store magnate. The story is told that Selfridge spent £2 million on his Dolly between 1924 and 1931. One night, she lost £80,000 gambling. To console her, he sent her a diamond bracelet and a rope of pearls that said, "I hope this will make up for your losses last night, darling."

A CASTING OF COUCHES

Marion Davies was the mistress of William Randolph Hearst, who supported her unsuccessful career as a movie actress. When an adviser suggested to Hearst that there was money in the movies, he replied, "Yes, mine."

PINNING

In the '40s, '50s, and '60s, a high school girl would rather die than admit to not being pinned by the football captain or, if he was taken, ANY BOY who would let her wear his pin. Pinning meant that they were "sorta going together." But as boys rarely honored this contract, she would end up "giving his pin back," which sometimes meant that she threw it at him in the cafeteria.

It was never the intent that the fraternity pin have a romantic implication. In the 19th century, the fraternity pin was given as a token of the privilege of admission into an exclusive, all-male brotherhood made up of members of similarly elite social status living together on a university campus. As women appeared in greater numbers on the college campuses, the young men thought of how a fraternity brother could invite the woman of his dreams into his fraternity family. The giving and receiving of the pin implies that the couple is almost engaged.

VALENTINE, WILL YOU BE MINE?

The custom of picking a valentine dates back to the Roman feast of Lupercalia, which began on February 15. Roman maidens would put their names into an urn. Each young man would draw a name and spend the year courting the girl whose name he had drawn, often writing love notes as part of the wooing ritual.

There are at least eight St. Valentines, and the saintly connection with the feast is extremely tenuous. Some people think the word is actually a corruption of the Norman French *galantin*, meaning "gallant lover."

However, medieval folk certainly believed in a St. Valentine; they thought all birds chose their mates on February 14 and that people should do so too. It was common for loves to call each other "my sweet valentine."

The first known valentine card was sent in 1415 by a French prisoner in the Tower of London—to his wife.

BELIEVE-IT-OR-NOT DEPARTMENT

In 1988, 900 million valentines were exchanged in the United States—a rate that has been constant throughout the last decade.

LOVE AT FIRST BYTE

Using a computerized bulletin-board system, people can now become friends with total strangers without actually meeting face to face until they are sure they want to. A computer-age variation of the old pen-pal relationship, this new romantic tool requires only that you have a telephone, a modem, a computer, and the money to subscribe to the dating board service—and that you can type.

Not a day passes that I have not loved you. Not one night that I have not clasped you in my arms.

NAPOLEON TO JOSEPHINE

A GIFT OF LOVE

It was Milton Glaser, the renowned graphic designer, who gave the nation a unique gift: I ♥ New York. This symbol has become a declaration of love for cities, states, and just about anything a heart could desire.

CHAPTER 3

SEX

Sex is the one part of love we think we can understand and explain the workings of. But even though we have substituted sex education in schools for the basic knowledge all primitive peoples acquire and accept from their earliest years, the facts of life still have the power to overwhelm us.

The man's courage is loved by the woman, whose fortitude again is coveted by the man. His vigorous intellect is answered by her infallible tact. Can it be true, as is so constantly affirmed, that there is no sex in souls? I doubt it exceedingly.

SAMUEL TAYLOR COLERIDGE

THE BIRDS, THE BEES . . .
BUT NOT THE BRITS

Title of a long-running play in the swinging London of the '60s: *No Sex Please, We're British.*

MOUTH-TO-MOUTH
RESUSCITATION

The longest kiss on film was performed by Regis Toomey and Jane Wyman (the first Mrs. Ronald Reagan) in a movie called *You're in the Army Now*, released in 1940. The kiss lasted 185 seconds.

The longest kiss on record that was *not* performed for a movie was accomplished in 1984 in Chicago, when Eddie Levin and Delphine Crha kept their lips pressed together for 17 days and 10-1/2 hours.

The longest kiss under water was achieved in Tokyo in 1980, by Toshiaki Shirai and Yukiko Nagata, on Fuji TV. Their aquatic amour lasted 2 minutes 18 seconds.

HOW LONG DOES LOVE LAST?

One estimate: two years is the natural life of an intense love affair, just long enough for the pair to produce a baby. Then the pair bond enlarges and naturally becomes a three-way relationship.

BABY, IT'S COLD OUTSIDE

In colonial America, courtship was always difficult. Houses and villages were miles apart, and a young man who had come courting could not in all charity be sent home in the dark at night. Thus arose the custom of inviting the young man to stay over. He slept in the same bed as his sweetheart, but they placed a long board between them. Couples were on their honor to respect the division represented by the board. Since in most frontier situations, an entire family slept in one room, the couple were under more or less constant supervision. However, it has been said that this custom gave birth to some of the healthiest whelps in the colonies.

Bundling, as it was called, was universally practiced for more than a hundred years. Unfortunately, improved public transportation put an end to the custom.

WHY THE HEART?

But if it all happens in the brain, why do we ascribe it to the heart? Perhaps because of the immediate quickening of the heartbeats, the feeling of palpitations, or breathlessness in the chest? and when we approach the loved one, that first touch is like holding on to a live wire, yet there is no actual exchange of electricity. It's all in the brain—or is it the heart after all?

DOUBLE TROUBLE

There used to be a rule in the movies that you could never show a couple actually *in* a double bed. Throughout the '30s, '40s, and '50s (the voluntary movie censorship system known as the Hays Code was not finally abandoned until 1966), married couples in American films always slept in twin beds, and any double bed, however rumpled, had to have only one occupant.

THE NOSE KNOWS

Our sense of smell is more acute than we know. Each of us has an individual scent, which is yet another way that siblings and parents recognize each other, although we may rarely be aware of it. Scientists believe that body scent is nature's way of enforcing an incest taboo, preventing us from becoming sexually attracted to members of our immediate family group.

Sex has become one of the most discussed subjects of modern times. The Victorians pretended it did not exist; the moderns pretend that nothing else exists.

BISHOP FULTON J. SHEEN

FALLING IN LOVE, NEUROLOGICALLY SPEAKING

The feeling begins deep within the brain in the hypothalamus, a pea-sized cluster of nerves that weighs only a quarter of an ounce. It is this tiny center that monitors the body's physical and emotional responses to the world.

When you find someone attractive, the hypothalamus sends a chemical message to the pituitary gland at the base of the brain, which at once releases hormones into the bloodstream. These almost instantly reach the sex glands, which immediately start producing more hormones—estrogen, progesterone, and testosterone. You start to feel tingly and slightly light-headed, and your heart starts beating faster. The entire process takes just a fraction of a second.

KISSING IS NOT ONLY FOR COUSINS

It is thought by thoughtful anthropologists that the act of kissing lips or cheeks or of rubbing noses is the long outcome of our first sniffing our prey, our food, or a potential mate before making too much of a commitment to move ahead.

LOOK D-E-E-E-P INTO MY EYES . . .

Deadly nightshade, a climbing vine with black berries, is a weed that grows in many backyards. Although the berries are poisonous, their juice was once used as a cosmetic. Italian women put drops in their eyes to dilate their pupils. *Atropa belladonna*, a drug derived from the roots, is used by opthalmologists for the same purpose today.

While belladonna (which means "beautiful lady" in Italian) is not itself an aphrodisiac, its effect on men cannot be ignored. The attentive gaze of a woman with large, dark eyes must have encouraged many to take romantic action.

WHAT'S UP, DOC?

Your mother may have told you that eating carrots would give you curly hair and sharp teeth, but according to Harry E. Wedeck in his *Dictionary of Aphrodisiacs*, among Arabs, carrots are eaten to enhance sexual desire.

HIGH IN THE SKY

One sign of falling in love is a high feeling similar to that of an amphetamine boost, according to Dr. Michael R. Liebowitz of Columbia University. The brain releases a chemical, probably phenylethylamine, that acts like stimulant, summoning up extra energy, boosting the heart rate, and making the world look great. People get hooked on it.

When you break up with your loved one, the crash has a lot in common with drug withdrawal. And many people assuage their distress by eating much larger than usual amounts of chocolate—which also contains phenylethylamine.

IS LOVE BLIND?
OR IS IT THE PHEROMONES?

We're always falling in love with the wrong person—in literature and in life. Animals have an easier time of it: they are attracted by chemical substances called pheromones that are secreted at the appropriate times for mating. Humans exude pheromones, too, but we have such Puritan prejudices about being clean that we mask them with deodorants or barriers of perfume.

Power is the great aphrodisiac.

HENRY KISSINGER

Sex without love is an empty experience,
but as empty experiences go, it's first-rate.

WOODY ALLEN

CHAPTER 4

LOVE WON
AND LOST

With the phrase *Significant Other*—which we sometimes reduce to *S.O.*—we thread a path through the thicket of possibilities in modern love en route to the truly Significant One. Are S.O.'s any different from L.O.'s (Love Objects)? Read on—and decide.

TRUST ME

The playwright George Bernard Shaw and the great actress Ellen Terry were passionate pen pals for eight years. Terry, though, always refused to allow a face-to-face meeting to take place because, she said, "I can't compete, 'cos I'm not pretty." Eventually the letter writers did meet. Terry was right. Shaw was disappointed, and the correspondence ceased.

As Shaw pointed out to all who would listen, "The ideal love affair is one conducted by post!"

SHORT BUT SWEET

Rachel, who had a reputation as one of the most remarkable Parisian actresses of the last century, was also renowned for her love affairs.

After seeing her act one evening in the 1840s, Prince de Joinville sent her his card with the words: "Where? When? How much?"

Her reply: "Your place. Tonight. Free."

HOW TO SAY PLEASE

The Wall Street Journal has uncovered a study conducted at the University of Louisville by the psychologist Michael Cunningham. "What," asked curious Michael, "is the best way to start off on the right foot?" After the academics puzzled, probed, and asked searching questions, the answer emerged. Just be yourself.

IT'S AN IDEA

When the *femme fatale* Sophie Arnould of the 18th-century Opera Comique wearied of her titled lover, she dispatched to his wife everything he had given her: jewels, coach—and children.

WORLDWIDE FLIRTING BEHAVIORS

As observed and noted by Dr. Irenaüs Eibl-Eibesfeldt, of the Max Planck Institute, Munich:

- Giving the person a slight smile and a bashful look, lowering the eyes, then turning them away. This is a pattern that may be repeated several times.
- Holding the person's gaze for just an instant longer than necessary.
- Making small touching movements.
- Letting the hand rest briefly on some part of the person's body.
- Moving closer than usual.
- Keeping the mouth slightly open, while looking unconsciously at various parts of the other person's body.
- Nodding the head in agreement, whatever the other person says.
- Facing the other person head on.
- Using the hands more than usual to emphasize points.
- Checking frequently to see how the other person is reacting to what is being said, usually by raising the eyebrows and opening the eyes very wide.
- Moistening the lips frequently.
- Making an effort to find subjects of conversation on which both parties are likely to agree.

THE RULES OF COURTLY LOVE

The idea of courtly love grew up in the 12th century, a time when all marriages were arranged, often between people who barely knew each other. Most aristocratic women felt only a sense of duty toward their husbands and wanted to be able to give affection freely. Troubadours traveled from castle to castle, singing about romances that were based on the Rules of Courtly Love that follow. The rules originated at the court of Countess Marie of Champagne. Her chaplain wrote them down in one book in a series called *Three Books About Love* that he produced (in Latin) to please her.

- Marriage is no real excuse for not loving.
- He who is not jealous cannot love.
- No one can be bound by a double love.
- Love is always increasing or decreasing.
- Boys do not love until they arrive at the age of maturity.
- When one lover dies, a widowhood of two years is required of the survivor.
- No one should be deprived of love without the very best of reasons.
- No one can love unless impelled by the persuasion of love.
- Love is always a stranger in the home of avarice.
- It is not proper to love any woman whom one would be ashamed to seek to marry.
- When made public, love rarely endures.
- The easy attainment of love makes it of little value; difficulty of attainment makes it prized.
- Every lover regularly turns pale in the presence of his beloved.
- When a lover suddenly catches sight of his beloved his heart palpitates.
- A man in love is always apprehensive.

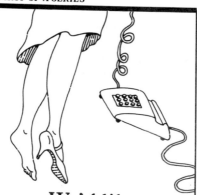

LOOKING FOR LOVE

South Seas island maidens used to advertise their availability by how they arranged hibiscus blossoms in their hair. Behind the left ear meant "I'm looking"; behind the right meant "I'm taken"; behind both ears meant "I'm taken, but I'm still looking."

"Louise, this is Larry Stolzer. Mr. Stolzer
has an extra ticket for King Tut."

CHANGING FASHIONS, 1988-STYLE

"The Touch of Your Hand on Mine" is all that's lacking for me right now. Do you feel the same? I'm a warm, intense woman in my 50s who loves to travel, converses fluently in Italian, French (and English). I long to visit museums and theaters with someone who can share my enthusiasm, and have affection and passion aplenty waiting for the right companion. I'm looking for someone special, about my age, who knows how to appreciate a mature woman as company, or as a friend, a lover, an intimate with whom to enjoy all that this wonderful world can offer. Can you feel the touch of that "special" hand in yours already? Appreciate a photo, please. Box ——.

CORRECT CONDUCT IN THE 1920s

Lady Troubridge decreed in her *Book of Etiquette*, written in 1926, "A public display of affection anywhere and at any time is not refined. Love is sacred, and its expressions should not be exposed to the rude comments of strangers. The young couple should conduct themselves with dignity, neither indulging in terms of endearment nor caresses, nor purposely ignoring each other."

Moving on to the engagement, Lady Troubridge has further advice for star-struck lovers: "If accepted, the well-bred man will immediately seek the girl's parents and acquaint them with the news, and express the hope that they will approve him as a son-in-law. At this point, if it has not already been disclosed, it is customary for him to reveal his status, financial and social, and to express himself ready to answer any questions that her parents may ask him. If he finds that he is not acceptable as a prospective son-in-law, he must explain his position calmly and carefully, making sure all the time to keep complete control of his feelings and not to allow himself to become either angry or impatient, remembering that while it is easy to make a quarrel it is not so easy to mend it, and as, naturally, his *fiancée* is fond of her family, any breach with them will not add to her happiness."

CHANGING TIMES

Good Form in England was a worthy book, written by an American observer and published barely a hundred years ago. "There is," he noted, "not one thing which will strike an American with such amazement as the indifference, disregard, and neglect with which women are treated in English high life. Daughters are expected to provide for themselves by "marrying well," which means catching a husband with money. It is not "good form" for a girl to show or expect any exhibition of love. The expressions "falling in love," "in love," etc. are thought "bad form" to use in conversation. Nor must a girl *think* even, much less talk, of a man's *looks*. As to his moral character or his physical condition, they are both of such secondary consequence, as to make them subjects quite unnecessary for consideration, if he have rank and titles, and he can make a handsome settlement on his wife. . . ."

Give me a dozen such heartbreaks if that would help me lose a couple of pounds.

COLETTE

MONEY TALKS

Being kept is not necessarily a bad deal, says Sylvia Porter in *Love and Money*. Take the case of two female friends from New York who met men when they were both in their twenties. One woman married her lover; the other could not because he was already married. But he set her up in a Manhattan apartment, which he bought in her name.

A decade later, both relationships had ended. And the divorcée moaned to her friend, "After eight years of marriage, I got a sofa and some dishes. But you got equity."

SARAH IN THE SKY

Sarah Bernhardt, the world-famous actress, had an astonishingly long list of lovers, all prominent men of the time. She also had an unrivaled talent for showmanship. She hired a hot-air balloon during a French world's fair, had the name of her current theatrical role painted on the basket, and circulated the rumor that she and her current lover were trying out love aloft. She was said to travel everywhere with a coffin made of rosewood and lined with white satin, supposedly large enough for two. And she autographed her photograph to a complete stranger with the words "To you, my dear, to whom I owe it all."

The worst thing an old man can be is a lover.

THOMAS OTWAY

MATCHMAKER, MATCHMAKER

You thought they only had matchmakers in *Fiddler on the Roof*? Not so. Rabbi Yeheskel Lebovic of Morristown, N. J., and his wife, Pearl, run a matchmaking service called Likrat Shiduch. Single Jewish men and women can subscribe for a one-time fee of $54.

Business is flourishing, with over 2,000 registrants on file. So far, the matchmaking service has resulted in over 200 weddings.

WANT TO DATE A NISSAN?

There's more than one way to meet your match when the expanding population of single Americans over 18 (68 million and counting) is your universe. Many dating services call themselves clubs, charge membership fees, screen applicants with care, and guarantee a certain number of introductions. Some focus on special clienteles, such as blacks, Asians, people of Hispanic origin, people with disabilities, people with graduate degrees, people with money . . . There's even a club for people who fancy the looks (or the cars) of those they pass on the road. They can get in touch via coded decals in their rear windows.

ANNIE: *Alvy, uh, let's face it. You know som—I don't think our relationship is working.*

ALVY: *Tsch, I know. A relationship, I think, is—is like a shark, you know? It has to constantly move forward or it dies. And I think what we got on our hands is a dead shark.*

WOODY ALLEN
Annie Hall

A LONG WAY TO JUMP?

A couple went to Coney Island to ride the Ferris wheel. It was their first date. The wheel got stuck, leaving them dangling at the high point. He proposed and she accepted. Or that's the story they tell their grandchildren.

If I had no duties, and no reference to futurity, I would spend my life in driving briskly in a post-chaise with a pretty woman.

SAMUEL JOHNSON

CHAPTER 5

TYING THE KNOT

Throughout history, marriages have been made for many reasons—political, economic, societal. Love was an afterthought at best. Until today. Now, no matter what other motives are also involved, we marry to give love a home.

There are usually months to anticipate all the major changes in our lives. The shortest of all transitions is the few moments that it takes to say, "I do."

Let me not to the marriage of true minds
Admit impediments. Love is not love
Which alters when it alteration finds . . .

WILLIAM SHAKESPEARE

MARRIAGE KNOTS, LOVE

The phrase "to tie the knot" goes far back
Roman brides traditionally wore a girdle, and part
of the marriage service, the bridegroom loosened it.
In a Hindu ceremony, the bridegroom knots a ribbon
around his bride's neck, and once it has been tied,
the bond is legal and cannot be dissolved. Members
of the Parsi sect in India tie a cord seven times
around the bridegroom's hands. In ancient Car-
thage, the couple's thumbs were laced together
with a strip of leather.

———

The truelove knot is an intricate, symmetrical arrangement, symbolizing equal affection. Lovers
gave each other rings, brooches, and bows tied in
truelove knots. Among Scandinavian nations, the
knot has always been the emblem of love, faith, and
friendship, symbolizing the strong ties of affection
and duty.

BRIDE PRICE

———

First marriages create a spending spree of nearly
$30 billion in the United States. In 1988, that amount
was spent on an estimated 5 million marriages, at
an average of a little over $10,000 per mutual con-
sent. However, if one takes into consideration the
number of couples who are married without any
pomp and circumstance, there is room for the
grandest of society weddings to cost $100,000 and
more. So the "average" cost of a wedding is some-
what misleading.

WEDDING TRENDS

- The average length of an engagement is almost a year, reports Barbara Tober, *Bride's* magazine editor-in-chief.
- The average age of today's bride is 23, and for the groom, it is 25.
- The average number of guests invited to the wedding reception is 200.
- Showers, the kind to which gifts are brought, are now being arranged for the bridegroom too.

HERE TODAY, GONE TOMORROW

To preserve the memory, unless you drop it, you can have your wedding invitation etched in crystal.

If permanence is not the goal, the bride can opt for a disposable paper wedding dress. To economize even further, a bride may buy a paper pattern and make her own gown. The pattern will cost about $5. A designer gown on the other hand can cost $3,500 (and very much more).

LUNE DE MIEL

In a 1987 survey of 3,700 readers, *Modern Bride* discovered that nearly 60 percent of the newlyweds planned to spend their honeymoon abroad.

The average length of time for a honeymoon is eight days.

Far more couples fly to their honeymoon destination than drive. "Just Married" signs may be fast disappearing.

WORLD'S LONGEST COURTSHIP

According to the Old Testament, Jacob labored seven years to be allowed to marry Rachel. At the end of this time, he was forced to marry Leah, Rachel's older sister. After another seven years, Jacob and Rachel were married, at long, long last.

WORLD'S SHORTEST COURTSHIP

Sir Harry Smith, a British officer, and his wife, Juana, were married in 1812 after the siege of the city of Badajoz, Spain, during the Peninsular War. She was a local girl of 14 who had sought his protection from pillaging British troops. He fell in love with her on the spot and married her the next day. They had a long, happy life together, ending in South Africa, where he became governor and she gave her name to the town of Ladysmith.

HOME SWEET HOME

Retail stores are reporting that many young couples, unable to afford the cost of a home, are buying and putting on display the very top of the line of crystal, china, and silver, and other evidences of conspicuous consumption.

Surveys show that about 63 percent of new brides plan to continue their careers and hope to have children too. Only 26 percent view their life goal as settling down and nurturing husband and children. This last figure has dropped 10 percent in the last 10 years, and all indications are that more and more women will be returning to work before their children's first birthdays.

Ten years ago, the average combined earnings of a couple when they were married was $17,600. That figure rose dramatically to an average combined income in 1987 of $40,800.

A CURMUDGEON'S VIEW

Q: What's the best time to get married?
A: For the young, not yet. For the old, not at all.

HOW OLD ARE YOU?

It was the custom in ancient Greece for a woman to give her age based on the number of years she had been married. The assumption was that her life did not begin until the day of her marriage.

DANCING ON NEWLY DUG GRAVES

On the frontier, people married young and spouses who died were speedily replaced. Weddings (and funerals) were the only gatherings that were not accompanied by work of some kind. As a result, these were great meeting grounds for young people and occasions for storytelling, eating, drinking, dancing, and courting.

MODERN TIMES

The country music singer Loretta Lynn was only 13 when she met Doolittle and soon after married him. In *Coal Miner's Daughter*, the full story is told: "Doolittle came over and said he had a big paycheck that day from working in the mines. He said we might as well get married the next day since he had the money. I thought if he asked me, I might as well get married. So I said yes.

"I remember Mommy's Cherokee father, Nathaniel Ramey, rocking on the front porch. He never said much but he looked at Doolittle and said 'You be good to my little girl, or I'll kill you.' Doolittle seemed impressed, because he knew that Indians never make promises they don't keep."

WE AWAIT WORD OF
AN 80TH ANNIVERSARY

In Alabama, New Hampshire, Texas, and Utah, a couple can be legally married at the age of 14. Thus, if both spouses of a couple married at age 14 live to be 100 (there are already 25,000 Americans over a century old), they could expect to celebrate their 80th wedding anniversary. The 50th anniversary is the one that is golden. The 60th is the diamond anniversary. The 80th . . . ?

ACCORDING TO BOSWELL,
THE BIOGRAPHER

"A gentleman who had been very unhappy in marriage married immediately after his wife died: Dr. Johnson said, it was the triumph of hope over experience."

THE BUSINESS OF MARRIAGE

"Love is an invention of the 12th century," said a French philosopher. For centuries, marriage was primarily a business arrangement everywhere in both the civilized and so-called primitive worlds. The "deals" were put together on the basis of land and other tangible property. *Real* estates, so to speak. The bride and groom often were just children or were very ill-matched in age. Frequently, they were complete strangers to each other.

Their exchange of vows was a sacred contract that could be broken only by death. Love was to be found in their relationship with God, not each other. The stork brought the children.

THE PRENUPTIAL CONTRACT

More and more frequently, couples are drawing up legal documents in the form of prenuptial arrangements, spelling out exactly the division of assets if the marriage does not last. As life expectancy has increased so dramatically in the last 25 years, people are beginning to view long-term commitments differently. There are now serial careers, serial marriages, and more mergers of families. The wedding contract is viewed by some as being similar to an employment contract or the purchase of a home. When the circumstances change, the contract is terminated and new settlements and arrangements are made.

Couples decide in advance who is to have the house, the dog, and the children, who is to get the alimony, the canary, and the gifts given by mutual friends. They agree who is to walk away with the jewelry they gave each other, the tape collection, and the exercise equipment. They agree to support each other until one or the other is unsupportable.

JUNE BRIDES

In past times, there were closed seasons during the year when the Roman Catholic Church decreed that marriages were not appropriate and could not be celebrated. The major times of abstinence, of course, were during Lent and Easter, and the tradition of June weddings may date from the rush to be married after Trinity Sunday, when all the fasting turned to feasting.

The notion that more weddings in the United States take place in June than in any other month may not always be true. If August has five Saturdays in the month and June has only four, there will be more August weddings. Generally speaking, though, there are more weddings in June—roughly, 276,000. In order, the most popular months for weddings after June are August, September, and October. January, February, and March have the fewest weddings.

MARRY ME

Legal citizenship is as valuable as currency in the United States, and it is well known that many illegal aliens have married solely in order to receive papers that allow them to remain in the country and obtain work. Questionable as these arrangements may be, they are rivaled by some sharp practices of the past.

In the 18th century, English law decreed that, on marrying, a husband acquired not only his wife but also all her money and worldly goods. Equally, he became fully responsible for any debts she might bring with her. Couples sometimes resolved this problem symbolically: the indebted bride came to church in her wedding gown, then stripped to her underclothes to be married "in her smock"—with nothing at all.

At one New England ceremony, the lady stood, quite naked, inside a closet, with her hand protruding through a circle cut in the door. Once the ring was on her finger, she quickly dressed in her bridal outfit (which the groom had thoughtfully placed in the closet) and came out, beaming and debt-free.

A more cynical solution to the problem of debts was for the burdened lady to call on a condemned man just before he was to be hanged, bringing with her a minister. After a hasty and none-too-sentimental marriage, the husband would go on to his appointment with destiny, and the widow's obligations would die with him. She *may* have promised to give a token of her appreciation to the family of her dear departed.

HIGHER EDUCATION FINALLY PAYS OFF!

Surveys used to show that women with a college degree were less likely to find mates than women who had only completed high school. Now the Census Bureau reports the situation has reversed itself, and 58 to 66 percent of college-educated women 30 and older can expect to be married by the age of 65, nearly 10 percent more than women who have only a high school diploma. Higher living standards may well be the reason: families these days need two salaries to support them, and a degree makes a woman more desirable—it brings better pay.

MAY I HAVE YOUR HAND?

Among gentlemen, a handshake is deemed to be as good as a written contract. "Shaking hands on it" is the demonstration of the acceptance of a verbal arrangement. The symbolic joining of right hands after the recitation of the wedding vows expresses not only the union of the bride and groom but also the father's "handing over" or "giving away" of his daughter to his son-in-law. Even before the ceremony takes place, the family of the bride must formally approve the marriage because it is they who send the invitations to the wedding guests—and foot the bills for the wedding!

I feel about marriage the way some people feel about cabbage, or like I feel about milk. It's a good product, but it ain't good for everybody.

RAY CHARLES

THE BEST MAN CARRIED A CLUB

It seems the best man once served a useful purpose. Warriors who wanted a bride of their own set out with their companions to wrest the bride from her original groom. Scandinavians were known to hold wedding ceremonies after nightfall, hoping the cover of darkness would afford some safety against surprise attack. For added protection, lances and torches were secreted behind the high altar. The best man was at the ready to protect the wedding party. Today, all he has to do is look decorative, remember the ring, and be nice to the plainest bridesmaid.

THE MARRIAGE.

IN THE RIGHT SPOT

The reason the groom stands to the right of his bride during the solemnization of the marriage vows is to protect his mate. In dangerous times, when unmannerly beasts—or even the family of the bride—may have tried to snatch away the beauty, the groom and the best man could reach for their swords, passing the right hand to the left hip, and be immediately ready for action.

I gravely doubt whether women were ever married by capture. I think they pretended to be [captured]—as they still do.

G.K. CHESTERTON

DID SHE REMEMBER TO WEAR SOMETHING BLUE, TOO?

Anne of Brittany is reputed to be the first bride who dressed entirely in white, for her marriage in 1498 to the King of France, Louis XII. Until then, brides would customarily either wear their best dress or whatever color they thought was the most becoming. Yellow and red were much in favor, but green was avoided because of its association with jealousy. Some brides even wore black and, in many cultures, highly decorated, bejeweled gowns.

It was once a major public declaration of wealth to wear a dress for only one day. "Look at that girl," a proud Industrial Revolution-era daddy is said to have said, "three hundred pounds on her as she stands."

THE WEDDING RING

More men are wearing engagement and wedding rings, and, says the Diamond Information Center, 73 percent of brides hope for and receive a diamond ring. Insurance on all jewelry is escalating so rapidly that very soon the cost of maintaining the insurance premiums will exceed the original price of the diamond.

There are two interpretations of the symbolism of a ring. One concerns the significance of the circle, which has no beginning and no end, and which implies the bond of love will last until eternity. The other interpretation is more sinister. The wearing of the ring is tangible proof that the man owns his wife just as a slave is owned by its master. The slave is chained with a circle, too: an iron manacle, allowing him just enough freedom to perform his work. There may be more to double-ring ceremonies that first meets the eye.

STRAIGHT FROM THE HEART

The custom of wearing the wedding ring on the fourth finger of the left hand originated in ancient Rome, where it was believed that "the vein of love" ran straight from that finger to the heart.

Every bride has to learn it's not her wedding but her mother's.

LUCI JOHNSON NUGENT

THE WEDDING VEIL

The original intent of the bridal veil was to depict modesty, chastity, and submission. Only the husband was allowed to feast on the beauty of his bride. It also imparted an element of suspense. When the marriage was an arranged one, the groom might not always have been happily surprised by the first glimpse of his new wife.

A WEDDING BREAKFAST

THE MARRIAGE BREAKFAST

In modern times, the wedding feast rarely is held at breakfast time but rather in the middle of the day or in the evening. It is a time when special, exotic (and, by extension, expensive) foods are shared between the families of the bride and groom and their guests.

In *Consuming Passions*, the authors, Peter Farb and George Armelagos, describe the wedding feast of the Trobriand Islanders, which is mirrored in Western society. First, there is the dinner offered by the family of the bride—the rehearsal dinner. This is followed by the exchange of gifts: the dowry from the bride and engagement ring from the groom, the giving of gifts to the wedding party, the offering of gifts to the couple from family and friends, and then the gift of the ceremony from the bride's family indicating its consent to the marriage.

BEER FOR THE BRIDE

Ale was once the accepted drink for special events, but to distinguish it from the everyday brews, special beers were fermented. Bride ales, or "bridals," were made for weddings, just as the universities have their own college ales—or "collegials."

THANKS, I'LL JUST HAVE A TASTE OF YOURS

Eating or drinking from a shared vessel, or sharing a morsel of wedding cake, is the symbolic farewell as the young couple are initiated from a society of unwed, young members of the group into the society of elders. Though the newlyweds remain part of the community, their roles are acknowledged to have changed.

THE FRUITCAKE WEDDING CAKE

Today, many fashionable couples choose to have carrot cake or chocolate cake for their wedding cake. They may be missing the significance of the tradition of having a fruitcake aromatic with cinnamon, cloves, and ginger. At the time of the Crusades, spices were so scarce and so prohibitively costly that they were saved for wedding and Christmas cakes. When spices were added to the wedding cake, the omens were good that the future would be prosperous—and fruitful. The multilayered cake represented the future generations that would be brought forth from this foundation.

Fruitcake—the customary wedding cake base— lasts, we all know, forever. Traditionally, it was covered with a dense layer of marzipan, and over all was troweled on a layer of concrete-like fondant icing. After the wedding, the cake was cut into tiny squares, which were placed in doily-lined miniature boxes, tied with ribbon, and sent to distant friends and relatives. On receiving the morsel through the mail, the recipient would sigh and place it safely in a drawer for a while. It is not known if anyone actually ate the cake.

A HANDFUL OF RICE

Rice is the symbol of fertility, and to throw rice at the just-married couple is a prayer that they will be blessed with children. But it can also be fatal to birds. Why? Birds eat the dry rice, which swells up in their stomachs.

Ecologically minded couples now request that they be honored with birdseed—but confetti serves the same symbolic purpose (provided the paper is biodegradable).

BIGGEST BIGAMIST

Giovanni Vigliotti, a flea-market vendor, was convicted of bigamy in 1983. During his 20-year career, he was married 105 times.

Marriage is popular because it combines the maximum of temptation with the maximum of opportunity.

GEORGE BERNARD SHAW

◇

POINTS OF REFERENCE

NEWSPAPERS AND MAGAZINES

Glamour
The New York Times

BOOKS

The Book of Etiquette. (1926).
  Lady Troubridge. The World's Work.
The Book of Insults, Ancient and Modern.
  Nancy McPhee. St. Martin's Press Inc.
Brewer's Dictionary of Phrase and Fable.
  Revised by Ivor H. Brown. Cassell.
The Bride: A Celebration.
  Barbara Tober. Harry N Abrams Inc.
A Celebration of American Family Folklore.
  Steven J. Zeitlin, Amy J. Kotkin, and Holly Cutting Baker.
  Pantheon Books Inc.
Crosbie's Dictionary of Puns.
  Harmony Books.
Curious Customs: The Stories Behind 296 Popular American Rituals.
  Tad Tuleja. Harmony Books.
Customs and Fashions In Old New England.
  Alice Morse Earle. Corner House Publishers.
Edward VIII.
  Francis Donaldson. Weidenfeld & Nicolson.
Extraordinary Origins of Everyday Things.
  Charles Panati. Perennial Library.
The Female Hero in Folklore and Legend.
  Tristram Potter Coffin. The Seabury Press.

Garden Flower Folklore.
   Laura G. Martin. The Globe Pequot Press Inc.
Good Form in England, by an American Resident in the United Kingdom. (1888).
   D. Appleton and Company.
Great American Folklore.
   Kent P. Battle, comp. Doubleday & Co.
The Great Lovers.
   Andrew Ewart. Hart Publishing Company.
Guinness Book of World Records.
   Alan Russell, ed. Sterling Publishing Co. Inc.
Henry VIII and His Court.
   Neville Williams. Macmillan Publishing Co.
The Human Animal.
   Phil Donahue. Simon & Schuster Inc.
The Illuminated Language of Flowers.
   Jean Marsh. Holt, Rinehart & Winston Inc.
The Language of Clothes.
   Alison Lurie. Random House Inc.
Love and Money.
   Sylvia Porter. William Morrow & Co. Inc.
Love Letters.
   Edited by Antonia Fraser. Alfred A. Knopf Inc.
The Oxford Dictionary of Nursery Rhymes.
   Iona Opie and Peter Opie. Oxford University Press Inc.
The Oxford Dictionary of Quotations.
   Oxford University Press Inc.
The People's Almanac.
   David Wallechinsky and Irving Wallace. Doubleday & Co.
A Proper Book of Sexual Folklore.
   Tristram Potter Coffin. The Seabury Press.
Pure Silver: The Second Best of Everything.
   David Reid and Jonathan Jerald. Harcourt Brace Jovanovich Inc.
The Royal Jewels.
   Suzy Menkes. Grafton Books.
Things Not Generally Known: A Book for Old and Young. (1857).
   John Timbs. David Bogue.
Wedding Album: Customs and Lore Through the Ages.
   Alice Lea Mast Tasman. Walker & Co.
Wedding Styles: The Ultimate Brides' Companion.
   Jules Schwerin. Prentice Hall Canada.
Womanlist.
   Marjorie K. Weiser and Jean S. Arbeiter. Atheneum Publishers.
The World Almanac of Facts.
   Mark S. Hoffman, ed. Pharos Books.

OTHER SOURCES

Hallmark Cards